D0593674

Serenity

Ariel Books

•

Andrews and McMeel
Kansas City

Serenity

Serenity copyright © 1994 by Armand Eisen. All rights reserved. Printed in Hong Kong. No part of this book may be used or reproduced in any manner whatsoever without written permission except in the case of reprints in the context of reviews. For information write Andrews and McMeel, a Universal Press Syndicate Company, 4900 Main Street, Kansas City, Missouri 64112.

ISBN: 0–8362–3081–7

Library of Congress Catalog Card Number: 93–73374

Paintings by Claude Monet

CONTENTS

For centuries, poets and philosophers have spoken of the universal desire for serenity—for those fleeting tranquil moments when the whirl of life slows down long enough for our blessings to come into focus. The electronic age has given us the ability to do more and more, faster and faster; at the same time, our need for a balance between work and leisure, action and reflection, has not diminished at all. In fact, since modern life is so fraught with stress and worry, our need for serenity has grown.

A quiet moment with a child, the satisfaction of a job well done, a chat with an old friend, a span of time alone to think and dream—serenity is a million different things to a million different people. Yet, fundamentally, it is the same for us all—the need for an uninterrupted slice of time in which we can appreciate the world around us and listen to the world inside us.

Gathered in this little volume are the thoughts of some who have addressed this need with wit, eloquence, and wisdom.

Acceptance

Do not seek to have everything that happens
happen as you wish, but wish for everything
to happen as it actually does happen, and
your life will be serene.

—EPICTETUS

The world is not to be put in order, the
world is order. It is for us to put ourselves
in unison with this order.

—HENRY MILLER

A new life begins for us with every second.
Let us go forward joyously to meet it. We
must press on, whether we will or no, and
we shall walk better with our eyes before us
than with them ever cast behind.

—JEROME K. JEROME

It is better to learn early of the inevitable
depths, for then sorrow and death take their
proper place in life, and one is not afraid.

—PEARL S. BUCK

God, give us grace to accept with serenity
the things that cannot be changed, courage
to change the things which should be
changed, and the wisdom to distinguish the
one from the other.

—REINHOLD NIEBUHR, *THE SERENITY PRAYER*

This one thing I do, forgetting those things
which are behind, and reaching forth unto
those things which are before.

—PHILIPPIANS 3:13

14

I know not how it is with you
I love the first and last,
The whole field of the present view,
The whole flow of the past.

One tittle of the things that are,
Nor you should change nor I—
One pebble in our path—one star
In all our heaven of sky.

—ROBERT LOUIS STEVENSON

Resolve, and thou art free.
>   —HENRY WADSWORTH LONGFELLOW

Were all the year one constant sunshine, we
>   Should have no flowers,
All would be drought and leanness; not a tree
>   Would make us bowers;
Beauty consists in colors; and that's best
Which is not fixed, but flies and flowers.
>   —HENRY VAUGHAN

Serene, I fold my hands and wait,
Nor care for wind, nor tide, nor sea;
I rave no more 'gainst time or fate,
For lo! my own shall come to me.

—JOHN BURROUGHS

I have come to the conclusion, after many
years of sometimes sad experience, that you
cannot come to any conclusion at all.

—VITA SACKVILLE-WEST

Coping

In the depth of winter, I finally learned that
within me there lay an invincible summer.

—ALBERT CAMUS

Do you know why that cow looks over that
wall?... She looks over the wall because she
cannot see through it, and that is what you
must do with your troubles—look over and
above them.

—JOHN WESLEY

20

COPING

All the irritations of daily life subject your mind and nerves and then your muscles to repeated tension. You can work out most of this tension with your exercise program, but if you are smart, you will try to avoid most of the tension to begin with.

—DR. LEON ROOT

Don't get your knickers in a knot. Nothing is solved and it just makes you walk funny.

—KATHRYN CARPENTER

21

SERENITY

He that can have patience can have what he will.

—BENJAMIN FRANKLIN

Perhaps, someday, even this distress will be a joy to recall.

—VIRGIL

If you can alter things, alter them. If you cannot, put up with them.

—ENGLISH PROVERB

We should be blessed if we lived in the
present always, and took advantage of every
accident that befell us, like the grass which
confesses the influence of the slightest
dew that falls on it; and did not spend our
time in atoning for the neglect of past
opportunities....We loiter in winter while
it is already spring.

—HENRY DAVID THOREAU

Sleep that knits up the ravelled sleave of
  care,
The death of each day's life, sore labor's
  bath,
Balm of hurt minds, great nature's second
  course,
Chief nourisher in life's feast.
              —WILLIAM SHAKESPEARE, *MACBETH*

What can't be cured must be endured.
              —FRANÇOIS RABELAIS

COPING

Great works are performed not by strength
but by perseverance.

—SAMUEL JOHNSON

O to be up and doing, O
Unfearing and unshamed to go
In all the uproar and the press
About my human business!
My undissuaded heart I hear
Whisper courage in my ear.

—ROBERT LOUIS STEVENSON

Though nothing can bring back the hour of splendor in the grass, of glory in the flower; we will grieve not, rather find strength in what remains behind.

—WILLIAM WORDSWORTH

Life is eating us up. We shall be fables presently. Keep cool: it will be all one a hundred years hence.

—RALPH WALDO EMERSON

Luck and strength go together. When you get lucky, you have to have the strength to follow through. You also have to have the strength to wait for the luck.

—MARIO PUZO

Keep a stiff upper lip.

—ENGLISH SAYING

All serious daring starts from within.

—EUDORA WELTY

Centering

Do not be in a hurry to fill up an empty
space with words and embellishments,
before it has been filled with a deep interior
peace.

—FATHER ALEXANDER ELCHANINOV

Life must be lived moment by moment.
Each moment carries a message, a lesson
for us.

—DR. DAVID K. REYNOLDS

Never put off enjoyment because there's no
time like the pleasant.

—EVAN ESAR

Our grand business undoubtedly is not to
see what lies dimly at a distance, but to do
what lies clearly at hand.

—THOMAS CARLYLE

Do not put off till tomorrow what can be enjoyed today.

—JOSH BILLINGS

For man, as for flower and beast and bird, the supreme triumph is to be most vividly, most perfectly alive.

—D.H. LAWRENCE

Life is too short to be small.

—BENJAMIN DISRAELI

A single moment of understanding can flood
a whole life with meaning.

—ANONYMOUS

Half the joy of life is in little things taken on
the run.

—VICTOR CHERBULIEZ

We know nothing of tomorrow; our business is to be good and happy today.

—SYDNEY SMITH

O solitude, the soul's best friend.
How calm and quiet a delight
   It is alone
To read, and meditate, and write,
By none offended nor offending none;
To walk, ride, sit, or sleep at one's ease,
And pleasing a man's self, none other to
   displease.

—CHARLES COTTON

Our continual mistake is that we do not
concentrate upon the present day, the actu-
al hour, of our life: we live in the past or in
the future; we are continually expecting the
coming of some special moment when our
life will unfold itself in its full significance.
And we do not notice that life is flowing
like water through our fingers.

——FATHER ALEXANDER ELCHANINOV

Simplicity

It is better to do the most trifling thing in the world than to regard half an hour as a trifle.

—JOHANN WOLFGANG VON GOETHE

To watch the corn grow, and the blossoms set; to draw hard breath over ploughshare or spade; to read, to think, to love, to hope, to pray—these are the things that make [us] happy.

—JOHN RUSKIN

38

SIMPLICITY

The day in its hotness,
The strife with the palm;
The night in her silence,
The stars in their calm.
                            —MATTHEW ARNOLD

I have a simple philosophy. Fill what's
empty. Empty what's full. And scratch
where it itches.
                            —ALICE ROOSEVELT LONGWORTH

SERENITY

I love to walk the fields; they are to me
A legacy no evil can destroy;
They, like a spell, set every rapture free
That cheered me when a boy.
Play—pastime—all time's blotting pen
  concealed,
Comes like a newborn joy
To greet me in the field.

—JOHN CLARE

SIMPLICITY

Nothing prevents our being natural so much
as the desire to appear so.
——FRANÇOIS, DUC DE LA ROCHEFOUCAULD

You will find angling to be like the virtue of
humility, which has a calmness of spirit and
a world of other blessings attending upon it.
——IZAAK WALTON

Backward, turn backward, O Time, in your
  flight,
Make me a child again just for tonight!

—ELIZABETH AKERS ALLEN

It is the child's spirit, which we are most
happy when we most recover; remaining
wiser than children in our gratitude that we
can still be pleased with a fair colour or a
dancing light.

—JOHN RUSKIN

42

SIMPLICITY

Blesses his stars and thinks it luxury.

—JOSEPH ADDISON

Simply the thing I am shall make me live.

—WILLIAM SHAKESPEARE

Learn not to sweat the small stuff.

—DR. KENNETH GREENSPAN

43

Joy

My heart leaps up when I behold
A rainbow in the sky.

—WILLIAM WORDSWORTH

He who binds to himself a joy
Doth the winged life destroy;
But he who kissed the joy as it flies
Lives in eternity's sunrise.

—WILLIAM BLAKE

I have laid aside business, and gone a-fishing.

—IZAAK WALTON

46

Everybody has their ups and downs so I
decided to have mine between good and
great.

—DAVID HOOGTERP

All musical people seem to me happy; it is
the most engrossing pursuit; almost the only
innocent and unpunished passion.

—SYDNEY SMITH

Be happy. It's one way of being wise.

—COLETTE

Laughter is the joyous, universal evergreen of life.

—ABRAHAM LINCOLN

You were once wild here. Don't let them tame you!

—ISADORA DUNCAN

You have to sniff out joy, keep your nose to the joy-trail.

—BUFFY SAINTE-MARIE

JOY

Mirth is like a flash of lightning, that breaks
through a gloom of clouds, and glitters for a
moment; cheerfulness keeps up a kind of
daylight in the mind, and fills it with a
steady and perpetual serenity.

—JOSEPH ADDISON

I finally figured out the only reason to be
alive is to enjoy it.

—RITA MAE BROWN

Keep your face to the sunshine and you cannot see the shadow.

—HELEN KELLER

Rosiness is not a worse windowpane than
gloomy gray when viewing the world.

—GRACE PALEY

Never give way to melancholy; resist it
steadily, for the habit will encroach.

—SYDNEY SMITH

Now each creature joys the other
Passing happy days and hours;
One bird reports unto another
By the fall of silver showers;
Whilst the earth, our common mother,
Hath her bosom decked with flowers.

—SAMUEL DANIEL

Contentment

The year's at the spring,
And day's at the morn;
Morning's at seven;
The hillside's dew-pearled;
The lark's on the wing;
The snail's on the thorn;
God's in His heaven—
All's right with the world!

—ROBERT BROWNING

CONTENTMENT

My crown is in my heart, not on my head;
Not decked with diamonds and Indian stones,
Nor to be seen: my crown is called content;
A crown it is that seldom kings enjoy.
—WILLIAM SHAKESPEARE, *HENRY VI*

Learn the sweet magic of a cheerful face;
Not always smiling, but at least serene.
—OLIVER WENDELL HOLMES

Is it so small a thing
To have enjoyed the sun,
To have lived light in the spring,
To have loved, to have thought, to have
  done;
To have advanced true friends, and beat
  down baffling foes?

—MATTHEW ARNOLD

Accept things as they are, not as you wish
them to be.

—NAPOLEON BONAPARTE

CONTENTMENT

Let us not therefore go hurrying about and
collecting honey, bee-like, buzzing here and
there impatiently from a knowledge of what
is to be arrived at. But let us open out
leaves like a flower…budding patiently…
and taking hints from every noble insect
that favours us with a visit.

—JOHN KEATS

People are always good company when they
are doing what they really enjoy.

—SAMUEL BUTLER

SERENITY

I want death to find me planting my cabbages.
—MICHEL EYQUEM DE MONTAIGNE

How many cares one loses when one decides
not to be something, but to be someone.
—COCO CHANEL

I am weary of swords and courts and kings.
Let us go into the garden and watch the
minister's bees.
—MARY JOHNSTON

CONTENTMENT

Prayer is the peace of our spirit, the stillness of our thoughts, the evenness of our recollection, the seat of meditation, the rest of our cares and the calm of our tempest. Prayer is the issue of a quiet mind, of untroubled thoughts.

—JEREMY TAYLOR

One thing is certain, and I have always known it—the joys of my life have nothing to do with age.

—MAY SARTON

Like a cat asleep in a chair
At peace, in peace
And at one with the master of the house,
    with the mistress,
At home, at home in the house of the living,
Sleeping on the hearth, and yawning
    before the fire.

—D.H. LAWRENCE

CONTENTMENT

The love of learning, the sequestered nooks,
And all the sweet serenity of books.
—HENRY WADSWORTH LONGFELLOW

Nothing can bring you peace but yourself.
—RALPH WALDO EMERSON

Affirmation

Know Thyself.

—SOCRATES

Every day, in every way, I'm getting better and better.

—ÉMILE COUÉ

Growth begins when we start to accept our own weakness.

—JEAN VANIER

AFFIRMATION

I didn't belong as a kid, and that always bothered me. If only I'd known that one day my differentness would be an asset, then my early life would have been much easier.

—BETTE MIDLER

The past exists only in memory, consequences, effects. It has power over me only as I give it my power. I can let go, release it, move freely. I am not my past.

—ANONYMOUS

The most visible creators I know of are those artists whose medium is life itself. The ones who express the inexpressible— without brush, hammer, clay, or guitar. They neither paint nor sculpt—their medium is being. Whatever their presence touches has increased life. They see and don't have to draw. They are the artists of being alive.

—J. STONE

Be your own palace or the world's your jail.

—ANONYMOUS

You grow up the day you have your first real laugh, at yourself.

—ETHEL BARRYMORE

The old woman I shall become will be quite different from the woman I am now. Another I is beginning.

—GEORGE SAND

If it makes you happy to be unhappy, then be unhappy.

—ANONYMOUS

It is easy in the world to live after the world's opinion; it is easy in solitude to live after our own; but the great man is he who in the midst of the crowd keeps with perfect sweetness the independence of solitude.

—RALPH WALDO EMERSON

Nobody can make you feel inferior without your consent.

—ELEANOR ROOSEVELT

AFFIRMATION

Even a slug is a star if it dares to be its horned and slimy self.

—JOHN HARGRAVE

Follow what you love! . . . Don't deign to ask what "they" are looking for out there. Ask what you have inside. Follow not your interests, which change, but what you are and what you love, which will and should not change.

—GEORGIE ANNE GEYER

69

If you can walk you can dance. If you can talk you can sing.

—ZIMBABWE PROVERB

Power is the strength and the ability to see yourself through your own eyes and not through the eyes of another. It is being able to place a circle of power at your own feet and not take power from someone else's circle.

—LYNN V. ANDREWS

I never saw a wild thing
Sorry for itself.
A small bird will drop frozen dead
From a bough
Without ever having felt sorry for itself.
—D.H. Lawrence

Why not be oneself? That is the whole
secret of a successful appearance. If one is a
greyhound, why try to look like a Pekingese?
—Dame Edith Sitwell

Reflection

Let us labour to make the heart grow larger
as we become older, as the spreading oak
gives more shelter.

—RICHARD JEFFERIES

A centipede was happy quite,
Until a frog in fun
Said, "Pray, which leg comes after which?"
This raised her mind to such a pitch,
She lay distracted in the ditch,
Considering how to run.

—EMMETT FOX

You should always know when you're shifting gears in life. You should leave your era, it should never leave you.

—LEONTYNE PRICE

Never hurry and never worry!
—E.B. WHITE (CHARLOTTE'S ADVICE TO
WILBUR IN *CHARLOTTE'S WEB*)

SERENITY

Work is not always required of a man.
There is such a thing as sacred idleness, the
cultivation of which is now fearfully
neglected.

—GEORGE MACDONALD

Do not let trifles disturb your tranquillity of
mind. . . . Life is too precious to be sacrificed
for the nonessential and transient. . . . Ignore
the inconsequential.

—GRENVILLE KLEISER

REFLECTION

I have said that the soul is not more than the
   body,
And I have said that the body is not more
   than the soul,
And nothing, not God, is greater to one that
   one's self is,
And I say to any man or women, Let your
   soul stand cool and composed before a
   million universes.

—WALT WHITMAN

Expecting life to treat you well because you are a good person is like expecting an angry bull not to charge because you are a vegetarian.

—SHARI R. BARR

Nature teaches more than she preaches. There are no sermons in stones. It is easier to get a spark out of a stone than a moral.

—JOHN BURROUGHS

REFLECTION

As a rule, for no one does life drag more
disagreeably than for him who tries to speed
it up.

—JOHANN PAUL FRIEDRICH RICHTER

Man can see his reflection only when he
bends down close to it; and the heart of
man, too, must lean down to the heart of
his fellow; then it will see itself within his
heart.

—JEWISH PROVERB

The text of this book was set in

Perpetua with display in Künstler Script

by Nylon Ink of New York City.

•

Book design by Liney Li